VERMONTERS
and the State
They're In

Books by Keith Jennison

Fiction

The Green Place
The Great International Novel Formula
From This to That

Nonfiction

Vermont Is Where You Find It
The Maine Idea
Dedication
New Hampshire
New York and the State It's In
Green Mountains and Rock Ribs
The Half-Open Road
The Boys and Their Mother
The American Indian Wars (with John Tebbel)
Remember Maine
The Humorous Mr. Lincoln
Yup . . . Nope and Other Vermont Dialogues
Year-Around Conditioning for Part-Time Golfers
        (with Dr. William A. Pratt)
New England in the Off-Color Season
Vermonters and the State They're In

Editor

The Essential Lincoln
The Concise Encyclopedia of Sports

VERMONTERS
and the State
They're In

Stories and Pictures

Arranged

by

Keith Jennison

The New England Press
Shelburne, Vermont

ISBN 0-933050-30-5
Library of Congress Catalog Card Number: 85-61316
First Edition

For additional copies, write:
The New England Press
P.O. Box 575
Shelburne, Vermont 05482

For Chris and Nick

in love and admiration

1

"What a beautiful day."

"Yes it is . . . for a town this size."

2

I ain't greedy for land . . .

all I want is what joins mine.

3

When I left the farm my father said the best advice he'd ever given me was . . .

never to walk barefoot and blindfold

across the barnyard.

4

Joe Marsh went around saying he was looking for a one-armed lawyer. When a friend asked him why, Joe said:

"I'm getting damn sick and tired of all the lawyers who say — on the one hand this, on the other hand that."

5

Many years back a Vermont storekeeper ordered a keg of molasses from an Albany wholesaler. The keg was damaged in transit and arrived empty. The storekeeper broke up the keg, started a fire with it in his stove, and threw the bill in the flames.

After six months of bills had been disregarded the wholesaler wrote the station agent asking if the keg had arrived. He wrote the president of the bank inquiring into the storekeeper's credit and sent a letter to the mayor asking the name of a good lawyer to start legal proceedings.

A few days later the wholesaler received the following letter:

Dear Sir: As station agent of this town I
can tell you the keg arrived. Molasses
didn't. As president of the bank I can
assure you that my credit is the best. As
mayor I have to tell you that I am the only
lawyer practicing in these parts. And if it
were not that I am the pastor of the
Federated Church I would tell you to go
to hell.

6

One of the town handyman's jobs was
to keep the memorial brass cannon on the
village green all polished up. He did
the job for eighteen years and one day
went to the selectmen and told them he
was quitting.

When they asked him why, he said, "I've saved my money and now I'm going to buy a brass cannon and go in business for myself."

7

A vacationing Texan, driving the backroads of Vermont, had to stop to let a farmer's cows cross the road. As the farmer passed in front of the Cadillac convertible the Texan called to the farmer, "How much land you got around here?"

"Wal," the farmer said, "on the pasture side of the road my land runs all the way down there to them alders along the brook. On the meadow side, over there, it stretches clean up to them larches on the hill."

The Texan studied the layout. "You know, pardner, I got me a spread in Texas and I can get in my pickup and drive all day without reaching any of my boundary lines."

"That so?" said the farmer. "I had a truck like that myself once."

8

When Walter Peabody got to be fifty he took a medical examination so he could get more life insurance. The doctor said he was in such good shape he'd okay him for any amount. Then he asked Walter what his father had died of.

"Who said he's dead?" Walter asked. "He's sixty-nine and does the chores right along with me."

The doctor asked the cause of death of his grandfather.

"Who said *he's* dead?" Walter said. "He's ninety-one, drives the tractor and works in the sugar house. More than that, next month he's going to marry a widow lady of thirty-three."

"Now why," asked the doctor, "would a man of ninety-one want to marry a woman of thirty-three?"

Walter said, "Who said he wanted to?"

9

After a few weeks in his new Vermont parish the minister said he had trouble getting his congregation to do any real hymn singing . . .

"It's almost as if they had to read every line before they sing it," he said, "to be sure they agree with what it says."

10

They say that money can't buy happiness
and maybe that's so . . .

but it sure can rent a lot of it.

11

"Do I think we're going to have another snowstorm?"

"Well, mister, the only people who predict weather around here are fools or strangers."

12

Art Benson, who did the town snow-
plowing, called the chairman of the Board
of Selectmen one morning at four o'clock
to tell him that the road commissioner
had died in his sleep.

"I'd like to take his place," Art said.

The chairman took a while to answer.
Finally he said, "If it's all right with the
undertaker it's all right with me."

13

"Can you tell me how to get to Green's Corners?"

"Don't you move a single damned inch."

14

"Who are you going to vote for at the Town Meeting, Ed?"

"I ain't made up my mind yet, but when I do I'm going to be damn bitter about it."

15

Sometimes I wonder if I have ten children or . . .

ASTINGS STORE
U.S. POST OFFICE
WEST DANVILLE, VERMONT 05873
HUNTING-FISHING
LICENSES SOLD HERE
INFORMATION

one child I have to tell the same thing to
ten times.

16

When one of the first automobiles in Vermont was driving on a back road it was sighted by a farmer and his son working in a field bordering the road.

"Jeezum Crow," the son said, "what's that?"

"Don't know," said his father, "but I better get my gun."

He ran to the cabin and came back with his shotgun. When "the thing" got close enough he let it have both barrels. The driver jumped out and ran back down the hill.

"Did you kill the varmint?" the son called.

"Nope," said his father, "but I sure made it let loose of the man it'd caught."

17

A Franklin County farmer had just finished putting a new tin roof on his barn when a tornado-like wind roared in, ripped off the roof and blasted it half a mile against the wall of a marble quarry.

A friend told him the Ford Motor Company would pay him money for scrap tin. The farmer crated up the wreckage and sent it along with a return address so Ford would know where to send the money.

He waited several weeks and finally got a letter from the Ford Motor Company. The letter read:

"We don't know what hit your car but we can't have it fixed until the middle of next month."

18

"Does this road go to Montpelier?"

"Well, it does . . .

and it doesn't."

19

At the end of a very moving sermon everyone's face in the congregation showed signs of tears except that of one man. When he was asked why he remained so unaffected, he replied:

"I belong to another parish."

20

One staunch Northeast Kingdom
Republican was examining a newly
minted half-dollar which displayed the
profile of John F. Kennedy. Turning it
over, he looked at the great seal of the
United States of America and said . . .

"I always knew they were on different sides."

21

When a newly elected representative was asked why she was a Democrat, she answered, "Because my husband is a Democrat and my father and grandfather were Democrats."

"Suppose," her inquisitor continued,

"that all your menfolk were damn fools.

Would that make you a damn fool too?"

"No," the woman replied, "it would make me a Republican."

22

One of the children of a fifth-generation Vermont family was born in Canada during his parents' ill-timed vacation.

As the boy grew up he was teased unmercifully by his older brother and sister for being a foreigner.

Finally his great aunt decided the persecution had gone far enough. She gathered the children together and told them she didn't want to hear any more of this ridicule.

"If a cat has kittens in the oven," she said, "they ain't biscuits." Then she fixed the tormentors with stern eyes. "And anyway, your brother was *made* in Vermont."

23

A Vermont wife, locally famous for the glazed ham she served to her dinner guests, allowed a friend to take notes on how she prepared the dish.

Her friend followed each step without question until the ham was in the roasting pan ready for the oven.

"I understand everything," the observer said, "except why you cut a little piece off the end of the ham before you put it in the pan."

"I don't know," the cook said, "that's the way my mother taught me to cook a ham."

"Let's ask your mother," the friend suggested. They drove to the mother's house and put the question to her. She said she didn't know either but that was the way *her* mother had taught her and suggested they go upstairs to ask her.

"Grandma," said the cook, "you started this whole bit about cutting a little piece off the end of your famous glazed ham before you put it in the oven. Why?"

"Simple," said Grandma. "My pan was too small."

24

A young couple built their house on a bare hillside. The neighboring farmer didn't speak to them until they started to plant little trees around their foundation. Then he walked over with a question.

"If you wanted to live in the woods, why didn't you build where they be?"

25

I got rid of my dizzy spells, but the damn doctor gave me so much medicine that I was sick for a long time after I got well.

26

Ed Richards lived on his farm close to the zigzagging New York State border. One day he was told that a new survey proved that he didn't live in Vermont after all — he lived in New York.

Ed said, "Well, thank the good God almighty, I couldn't of stood another of them Vermont winters."

27

A young man walked up to the crest of a hill overlooking a small Vermont village. At the top he met an old man resting beside a mountain spring. The young man looked down at the village and said, "What kind of folks live in the village down there?"

"What kind of folks lived in the village you came from?" asked the old man.

"They were the meanest bunch of bad-mouth gossips I ever knew," the young man said.

"That's just what they're like down there," the old man said.

The young man turned and started back to where he had come from.

While the old man still sat by the spring, another young man toiled up the hill. He too stopped at the spring and looked down at the village.

"What are the folks like who live down there?" he asked.

"What were they like in the town you came from?" the old man inquired.

The young man said they were the finest, friendliest, most generous neighbors a man could want.

"That's just what they're like down there," the old man said.

The young man thanked him and started down the hill.

Index and Picture Credits